Livi

GW00738231

Learning from the lives of

William Tyndale John Newton David Brainerd Eric Liddell

Kath Dredge

Illustrated by Colin Lumsden

DayOne

© Day One Publications 2001
First printed 2001

Scripture quotations are from The New King James Version.
© 1982 Thomas Nelson Inc.

British Library Cataloguing in Publication Data available
ISBN 1 903087 28 7

Published by Day One Publications
3 Epsom Business Park, Kiln Lane, Epsom, Surrey KT17 1JF.
☎ 01372 728 300 **FAX** 01372 722 400
e-mail sales@dayone.co.uk

Sub editor: Karen Roberts   Designed by Steve Devane.

Printed by CPD Wales, Ebbw Vale

Acknowledgements

I would like to thank my family and friends for their help, patience and advice. Special thanks to Sam Liu, my junior proof-reader, Phil Arthur, my senior one and Joan Murray whose original illustrations inspired the text.

Kath Dredge

May 2001

Contents

Opening the King's eyes

The story of pioneer translator **William Tyndale**

D o you have a Bible in your house? Have you been in a bookshop and seen all the Bibles you can buy? More than five hundred years ago there was not a single Bible written in English and the people had to rely on priests to tell them what the Bible said. The priests made up rules that were not in the Bible and many of the people did not know Jesus Christ as their saviour. A young man, named William Tyndale, struggled throughout his life to produce Bibles in English for anyone to read, knowing that the word of God should be available to everyone.

William Tyndale was born in Gloucestershire, England, in 1494, although little else is known about his birth. His parents were able to afford to send him away to be educated and when he was thirteen he was sent to Magdalen (pronounced 'maudlin') Hall, a school attached to the University College of Oxford. He studied at the University during his teenage years and the life of a student was very hard then. Days began at 5am in chapel, with a three-hour lecture beginning at 6am. A lunch break was followed by more lectures until 5pm when supper was served. The students were too poor to have candles and so would spend the hours afterwards talking about the things they were learning. In the evening they would run around for half an hour to get warm before getting into bed.

Life was definitely hard and the lectures were long and dull but it was an exciting time to be a student in Oxford. The Middle Ages were making way for the Renaissance (which means 're-birth'), when ancient writings had been discovered in Europe and the educated men there began to rethink many of their ideas, looking for the truth. Some of those men came to Britain and taught at

William studied at Oxford University during his teenage years

Oxford and Cambridge, awakening a real desire for learning and discovery among the students. Explorers like Christopher Columbus set sail to discover new lands, and artists such as Leonardo da Vinci and Michaelangelo were amazing people with their marvellous works of art. It had been unpopular for hundreds of years to move away from traditional ways of thinking but now scholars who rejected these traditions were in demand. Things that had always been accepted were now questioned.

The Church was very powerful in Europe and England, but was a poor representative of God. The bishops, priests and the Pope—who was then head of the Church—were very wealthy while many people were poor. These religious leaders were not allowed to marry but many of them had partners and children. They insisted the people had to behave well before God but did not do so themselves. Because printing had only just been brought to England very few people owned Bibles. The priests had Bibles in Latin and led the people to believe that they had to buy forgiveness from God, which was why the Church was so rich.

Scholars now began to speak out against the corruption of the Church. One of these was a Dutch man called Desiderius Erasmus, who worked hard to learn Greek so that he could study Greek manuscripts to find out what the Scriptures really said. He went to Queen's College, in Cambridge, to lecture in Greek, and while he was there he put together the New Testament showing Greek and Latin translations side by side. The Church leaders were angry with this, but very few people understood Greek so it did not seem too dangerous. At Cambridge, however, students bought Erasmus' translation and studied it and began to understand some of the wonderful truths about Jesus Christ. They realised that Jesus alone could forgive sins, and that the Church had no right to 'sell' forgiveness for money.

When William had finished his studies at Oxford he went to study at Cambridge, the only other university in England at the time. Erasmus left before William arrived but he had caused turmoil among the students and Cambridge became the University of Reformers, full of students who wanted to see the Church change and follow the Scriptures faithfully. William was present at many of the discussions about the Scriptures and the teachings of the Church and began to realise how important it was to really know what God had said. Books were now coming in from Europe, some written by the famous German reformer, Martin Luther, and the Church leaders began to see how dangerous the situation was becoming for them. Once the people knew what the Scriptures said they would no longer need the priests to tell them and the Church would lose its power, and its money. Cardinal Wolsey, the Chancellor of England and the King's highest adviser, was also the Archbishop of York, and when he heard that the universities were infected with 'Lutherism' he was very angry. Reformed books were banned and huge bonfires were made to burn the ones that were found and had been confiscated.

William spent his time at Cambridge reading, listening and studying. He loved reading the works of Erasmus, for he was a brilliant scholar, but he loved his Greek New Testament more than anything else. He could clearly see how far removed from the Bible the Church had become. Erasmus had pointed out the problems with, and failings of the Church but William was not content to just read and agree—he knew something had to be done about the situation before it became much worse.

Eventually, William decided to leave Cambridge. There were many discussions at the University but William felt that the situation needed more than words. He knew that he had to go away to be alone with God and find out exactly what God wanted him to do. He left Cambridge and returned to Gloucestershire.

God led William to Sir John and Lady Walsh, who needed a tutor for their two young sons, as children of wealthy families were taught at home in those days. William was welcomed into their home, Little Sodbury Manor, and found peace in his room on the third floor. He had been made a priest when he was twenty years old and so was able to preach in the church of St Adeline, on the hillside above the manor. When he was not preaching and not teaching the boys he would spend the time praying, reading and studying languages. He translated Erasmus' book, *Manual of the Christian Soldier,* into English and gave the copy to the Walsh family who were glad to have it and proud of their clever tutor.

William read more of the word of God and longed to share it with others. He would sometimes walk fifteen miles to Bristol and preach from the New Testament on St Austin's Green. His message was plain—turn from any wrongdoing and believe in Christ, for salvation is only found in him. Those who made their living by taking money from people and promising that this would help their sins be forgiven were, naturally, unhappy with William, and he was ordered to attend a Church Court. He was charged with offences against the Church and told that he could not rely on Sir John Walsh to protect him. He was finally allowed to return to the manor but now knew that he was in danger. Only a few years earlier people had been burnt to death for teaching their children the Lord's Prayer and the Ten Commandments in English. This shows how corrupt the Church was then, and how far from God they really were.

The Walsh family had many visitors and often Church leaders and priests would join the family and William for a meal. They would talk about the state of the country, the king, Henry VIII, and his court, wars overseas, the new ways of thinking and the Church. Some of the important Church leaders did not like William being there, for he was only a lowly priest and tutor, but Sir John loved to hear him joining in the talk, using words of Scripture to back up his arguments. During one discussion, a well-known churchman said to William: "It were better to be without God's law than the Pope's." There was a shocked silence after this

Work finally began on printing the New Testament in English

and William replied by saying: "I defy the Pope and all his laws. If God spare my life, before many years I will cause the boy that drives a plough shall know more of the Scriptures than you do."

It was very soon after this that William realised that he could not stay at Little Sodbury because it had become too dangerous. However, his clash with the churchman had been God's way of showing him what he must do. He would translate the Bible into English so that even a ploughboy could understand God's wonderful promises and the hope of salvation.

He faced an obstacle immediately because the law said that no one could translate the Scriptures without the permission of a bishop. William heard that Bishop Tunstall of London was a scholar and liked by Erasmus, and he decided to go and speak to him about his plans. After two years with the Walsh family he left Gloucestershire and made for London where unfortunately he faced disappointment. Bishop Tunstall was indeed clever, but not brave enough to help William, and sent him away. William was upset but not daunted. He knew God would help him find a way, for the Lord had people in many places and those in the city loved the truth and were not afraid to help reveal it.

William had to wait in London for several weeks before the Bishop would see him. While he was there he preached and a cloth merchant, called Humphrey Monmouth, heard him. He later heard that William had been turned down by the Bishop and invited him to his home. Once again William lived quietly, spending most of his time studying and preparing for the challenges ahead.

Among Humphrey's merchant friends were men from Germany who also loved the Reformation truths. At the dock where the goods were brought to land, Lutheran books were arriving in their hundreds. William read more of Luther's works and realised that he had more in common with Luther than he did with Erasmus. Erasmus saw the faults in the Church and wanted them put right, but Luther and William saw that the problem went further than that. The Church was not teaching what the Bible taught and therefore needed to be changed. The early Reformers had been forced out of the Church because they realised that the teaching could never be changed within the Church. The Reformers believed the Scriptures were the final test of all teaching. The Church should be judged on what they said according to the Bible, not the Pope.

William came to realise that there was nowhere in England where he could safely translate the Scriptures and get them printed. In 1524 he left England for Europe, and never returned home again.

He spent a short time in Hamburg, in Germany, and then travelled to Cologne, the centre of printing in northwest Germany. He found a printer, called Peter Quentel, who was willing to help him and work finally began on printing the New Testament in English. It was a slow and difficult job, because the printer had to pulp his own paper as well as setting up the metal type in the frame on the press. Unfortunately, a man called John Cochlaeus, who hated the Reformers, heard of their work and reported it to a senator of Cologne who immediately ordered the arrest of William and his helper, William Roye, and the capture of the paper and the type.

By God's grace, William and his friend heard of this and were able to grab the sheets they had printed and slip out of Cologne at night, before they were caught. They only had the gospels of Matthew and Mark by then but they sent these to England. The two men then fled to the city of Worms, where they found another printer, Peter Schoeffer, and they were able to continue with their translations. In England, the king and his advisors were more concerned with the disastrous harvest of 1525 and the increasing scarcity of food than about William and his troublesome work. In the spring of 1526, as England began to enter a state of famine, grain arrived from Europe, accompanied by the printed English New Testament. The people received food for their bodies and for their souls at the same time.

It was not long at all before the New Testament reached the hands of even the humblest people in England. It sold for half a week's wage for a labourer. Many people could not read, unable to afford the cost of education, and unable to afford a copy for themselves. Many joined in groups with friends and bought one copy that could be read to them. In this way God's word was heard and understood and loved.

The people who were angriest about this development were the men of the Church. Bishop Tunstall was furious and he and other bishops had an emergency meeting and decided that they would seek out every English copy of the New Testament, and burn it.

At St Paul's Cross in London, Bishop Tunstall preached against William and his work, and burnt a copy of the New Testament. When William heard of this he said: "In burning the New Testament they did none other thing than I looked for; no more shall they do if they burn me also, if it be God's will it shall so be. Nevertheless, in translating the New Testament I did my duty."

Despite this opposition more copies of the New Testament entered the country and the bishops decided their only course of action was to buy every copy they could and burn it. The printers were happy about this because they were making money and William was able to use the money to revise his earlier work, which was now being burnt. Cardinal Wolsey ordered a search of London, Cambridge and Oxford to find all the books. Many young men were arrested and sent to prison or taken to be burned, simply for owning a copy of the New Testament in English. One year after the New Testament had first arrived in England the prisons were overflowing with people from all walks of life whose only crime was to read the word of God in their own language.

Despite the constant danger he was in, William continued to

improve his work. He always remembered that he was writing for ordinary people and worded it so that anyone could understand it. He used words like 'under-captain' instead of 'centurion' and much of what he wrote was eventually used in the Authorised Version of the Bible, printed in 1611.

Cardinal Wolsey wanted to get rid of William far more than he did the copies of the New Testament. He sent instructions to John Hackett, the ambassador in Europe, to have William arrested, but after a month there was still no sign of him. Wolsey then sent a priest called John West to join the search but God kept William safe and his persecutors were unable to find him.

William had left Worms, alone, and found another printer, John Hoochstraten, in Marburg. John printed more of his work, including a book called *Parable of the Wicked Mammon*. Five months later he printed his best-known book, *The Obedience of the Christian Man*, which was his answer to the accusation that the Reformers were encouraging people to disobey their rulers. In his book he showed how a Christian seeks to live in a godly way in every part of his life, and do his best to be a good citizen. Henry VIII read the book and said it was a book all kings needed to read. This show of support, even from the King of England, did not stop the leaders of the Church from wishing to kill William, however.

William's next task was to translate the Old Testament from Hebrew into English. He was fluent in Hebrew, Greek, Latin, Italian, Spanish, French and German, able to speak any of these as well as his native English, which definitely made his task easier. He received visits from his close friend, John Frith, and he always remembered that he was doing God's work. He was now thirty-five and knew that the hunt for him was fiercer than ever. He finished the translation of the first five books of the Bible, known as the Pentateuch, and he decided to leave Marburg and get them printed somewhere else. He reached Antwerp, but knew that Cardinal Wolsey's men were already there so he instead caught a boat to

Hamburg where he hoped to find a printer. He thought a sea voyage would avoid a dangerous journey overland but as they sailed around the coast of Holland the ship was tragically wrecked and William's manuscripts were lost. Money, time and months of work were gone in a moment.

William eventually arrived in Hamburg, on another ship, and made his way to the home of the Emmersons, who were friends of his. He told the awful story to a friend from Cambridge, Miles Coverdale, and although William was disheartened by the loss, God used Miles to encourage him to start again. Nine months later the translation was ready for printing. Once it had been printed William returned to Antwerp, although he was no safer there than anywhere else.

The Pentateuch arrived in England in the summer of 1530. At the same time Henry VIII spoke against William's two books—that he had liked so much two years earlier—and Bishop Tunstall had another bonfire of books at St Paul's Gate. In the Low Countries, which are now Holland and Belgium, and in regions of Germany, the emperor, Charles V, ordered all copies of the New Testament to be burned and people who supported the Reformed teaching were all to be killed; men with a sword and women by being buried alive. God gave people strength during these terrible times to remain true to him, despite the evil carried out by their fellow man.

By the end of 1530 Cardinal Wolsey's zeal for finding William lessened slightly, because he was falling out of favour with the king. Henry wanted to divorce Catherine of Aragon and marry Anne Boleyn, a much younger and prettier woman, in the hope of producing a male heir for the throne of England. Divorce was against the Church's teachings and the king and the cardinal had come into conflict. Wolsey was worried about upsetting the king and being executed, but he was also frightened of falling out with the Pope because he wanted to keep England under the Pope's rule

The danger around William was never ending

and free from the teaching of the Reformers. He also nurtured a hope that he might one day be Pope himself. After months of difficulties Wolsey was stripped of all his wealth and importance and died at the end of November 1530, a shadow of the man he had once been.

King Henry decided to try a new approach in the efforts to find William. He sent Stephen Vaughan, a merchant adventurer of Antwerp, to find William and ask him to return to England to work for the king. Stephen searched for many months, without success, until William contacted him and agreed to meet him outside Antwerp. William told Vaughan about his difficult life, the constant hunger, thirst, cold and danger with which he lived, and that it was because he loved his king and country that he lived his life in such a way. Vaughan found that he liked William and saw in him a man of courage and honesty, who wanted to serve God faithfully above everything else. There was nothing Vaughan could say which would persuade William to return to England, despite his love for his country, and Vaughan eventually returned, alone.

William received news a little while later of the great troubles the Reformers were under. Some of his friends from University had been burnt to death while others, under torture, had signed papers denying their faith. William wrote kindly to those who had been mistreated, knowing how hard it was for them, and urging them to remain firm in Christ and pray for his strength to help them. He found it hard, knowing that it was his work that had caused so many people to be in danger from the authorities. However, he also knew that God's word was so precious, and the truths in it so important, that the Bible had to be made available to everyone, whatever the consequences. He knew that ordinary people needed to know of the Lord Jesus and put their faith in him as a saviour, and this could not happen without the Bible showing them who he was.

A new Chancellor of England was appointed, Sir Thomas

More, and he was quick to have anyone arrested who was suspected of holding Reformed views. He asked every prisoner if they knew anything of William. Sir Thomas was allowed to read the banned books and then wrote books of his own against them. He wrote several books on the subject, and the more he wrote the more the people became aware of William's views, and realised how right they were.

William's friend, John Frith, returned to England and was arrested and imprisoned in the Tower of London. He was given freedom to write from within his cell but he found it hard to be separated from his family. William wrote as soon as he heard, urging him to keep his faith in Christ, and reminding him that his wife was content that the will of God would be done. After five months imprisonment John Frith was burnt to death, and William grieved for the loss of a good and constant friend.

The danger around William was never-ending but there were a growing number of people who held Reformed views and were willing to help him. He was invited to live in the home of Thomas Poyntz, a relative of William's old employer Lady Walsh. Thomas was one of many English merchants trading in Antwerp who brought trade into the town and so were treated kindly by the town leaders. The merchants paid William well and for the first time in many years he was comfortable and quite safe. He was thin and weak by then but was welcomed by Thomas' family and gained strength from the good food he was provided with.

He used his time carefully while living with the Poyntz family. On Saturdays he would go into the town, looking for people who were hungry or homeless, and do what he could to help them. On Sundays he would go to the home of one of the merchants and read the Scriptures, in a way that the people listening found useful and comforting. Mondays were spent visiting and helping the English people who had been forced to leave England. The rest of the week he worked on his books and he was able to complete a revision of the New Testament and send it to England.

A young man called Henry Phillips was the one who would betray William. He had gambled away all of his money and was too scared to tell his father. He agreed to help kidnap William in the hope of earning some money. He approached the English merchants at Antwerp and, because he had a likeable air about him, was soon invited to their homes, and not long after that he met William. Phillips seemed so charming that William invited him back to Thomas' house and showed him his books. Thomas was not happy about the stranger but William assured him that Phillips held to their Reformed views. After a few days Phillips disappeared, riding straight to the town of Brussels, twenty-four miles away, where he gathered a small group of officers and then set off again for Antwerp.

Phillips called to see William, who invited him to lunch in the town. Phillips had so little sympathy for his victim that he asked William to lend him two pounds—enough for a poor family to live off for two months—claiming that he had lost his purse that morning. William lent him the money and they left the house together. In a narrow alley outside Phillips insisted that William enter first. As William walked forward Philips pointed at him and two men leapt out from the shadows, grabbed William and tied him up, making him a prisoner.

Thomas was furious when he heard the news and tried everything he could to free his friend, but there were too many people who had waited too long to have William let go that easily, and Thomas was put under house arrest to stop him bothering the authorities.

William was thrown into the state prison at the Castle of Vilvorde. It was a dreadful building with a moat, seven towers, three drawbridges and huge walls. He was put into a damp, dark and dirty dungeon but even there, with the little light he had, he continued his translation work. He frequently had visitors, and many of them tried to convince him to change his mind so that he would be set free, but he would not be moved. He wrote to the prison governor—and the letter still exists, written in Latin—asking for a lamp and some warmer clothes, because the cold and dampness of the cell had given him a bad chest and head.

After more than a year of captivity, William was taken out of his cell to the town square. He had his office as priest publicly taken away from him and his hands were scraped with a knife or shard of glass to show that he had lost the benefits he received when he was anointed. His priestly robes were taken from him and he was given ordinary clothes to wear. The Church had now dealt with him and he was handed over to the state, as the Church had no power to execute those it believed to be going against its teachings. William was taken back to his cell for another two months.

In October 1536, William was taken from the prison again, this time to the place of execution. He was asked again if he would give in but he knew he could not deny his God, and he pitied the people who were trying to make him do so. William was only forty-two. He had never married, had no children, and had been forced to keep away from his beloved England for the last twelve years. He knew that his sacrifices had been worth it because so many people now had access to God's word.

He was taken towards the chain and noose which would strangle him, and the logs and brushwood which would burn up his lifeless body, and he uttered one last prayer: "Lord, open the King of England's eyes."

Moments later William was strangled, but his death was not in vain, for many more brave men fought to continue printing the Bible in English. God answered William's final prayer. In the year of his death there were two English translations of the Bible available in England. One had been translated by William's friend, Miles, and the other was the work of John Rogers, a man converted to Christ in Antwerp while William was there. Both

Bibles used much of William's work, and were dedicated to the King of England. The king gave his agreement for the Bibles to be used, and ordered that every church in England should display "one book of the whole Bible of the largest volume in English."

It is easy to forget, with so many Bibles now easily available, how difficult it was to first produce it. God's word, however, is so precious and wonderful, that it needed to be made known to all the people, whatever the cost. The Bible must be treasured as the word of the Living God, and thanks given that we are all able to read it whenever we like.

From master to servant

The amazing life of John Newton

Winds of eighty miles an hour ripped through the ship, tearing away timbers and flooding cabins as the crew battled against the tempest, some trying to work the pumps and others trying to bail out the vessel. The ship's cargo was lighter than usual—making her more stable—but danger still lay in the huge waves that were flaying her mercilessly. One of the crew worked at the pump tirelessly from three in the morning until midday and as he pumped he found himself thinking of God and asking for his mercy. Even as he did so he was fearful that his life had up till then been too full of sin and evil for God ever to look upon him favourably. Less than an hour after he had gone for a well-earned rest he was called back to the deck to steer the ship until midnight, being too tired to exert himself physically. That man was John Newton, one of our best-loved hymn writers. With time to think, words from the Bible came into his mind and he realised what a terrible sinner he was. He wondered if it really was true that Jesus could save sinners as bad as he knew himself to be.

By six the following evening the ship was no longer in danger and Newton began to pray and give thanks and apologise, determined from that moment on to give his life to the Lord and turn his back on his dreadful past. He knew that God had had to punish him severely before he would learn to rely on him, and he realised how much God must care for him to have taken such time and effort over him. This impressed him even more when he reflected on his life and what a godless time it had been.

John Newton was born in 1725 in London and was very close to his mother. His father was captain of a trading ship and was often away for long periods of time. John had no brothers or sisters and

On his eleventh birthday John joined his father's ship and sailed with him for the Mediterranean Sea. John and his father seemed strangers and the small boy was afraid of this hard and strict man he barely knew.

his mother spent her time teaching him biblical truths and children's hymns, and praying that he might become a Christian, as she was and, if it were God's will, that he would become a minister too.

John had only eight short years with his mother before she died. His father was still away and John made friends with some boys who were a bad influence on him. His father soon remarried and John was sent to a boarding school in Essex. After years of being the centre of attention in his life with his mother it was hard for John to adapt to being one of hundreds of little boys. He did not do well in the two years he was at the school and began to forget everything his beloved mother had taught him.

On his eleventh birthday John joined his father's ship and sailed with him for the Mediterranean Sea. John and his father seemed strangers and the small boy was afraid of this hard and strict man he barely knew. He spent more time with the crew and learnt some shocking language and behaviour from them.

A couple of episodes occurred early on in his life to give him pause for thought about his attitude. When he was twelve he was thrown from a horse and badly shaken. He recalled his mother's words as he realised that he could have been killed and would then have had to stand in judgement before God—a frightening prospect already, even at his young age. For a time he tried to start afresh but this resolve did not last for long. A little while later, on a Sunday night, John agreed to go out with a friend, on his boat. For some reason John was late and the boat sailed without him but soon overturned and John's friend was drowned. At the funeral John thought again of his lucky escape and decided to try again to live a better life but this determination soon faded. John's teenage years were spent sailing backwards and forwards through Europe and the Mediterranean Sea, and the influence of the older sailors on him grew stronger and more destructive.

At the age of fifteen John suddenly became very religious, and began to pray and read his Bible. He stopped eating meat and seemed to be really sorry for his past wrong doing. He hardly dared speak for fear he would say the wrong thing, but this kind of zealous fervour actually made him very miserable. He bought a book by Lord Shaftesbury called *Characteristics of Men, Manners, Opinions, Times etc…* which he hoped would be helpful and he read it many times. Unfortunately a lot of what it said did not come from the Bible and John felt even worse. His mind was slowly being poisoned against the wonderful truths his mother had shared with him, long ago.

Two years later, when John was seventeen, his father decided he did not want to return to sea and had to quickly decide what he could do with John. A friend in Liverpool, Joseph Manesty, agreed to send John to Jamaica where young men were needed to look after slaves on the sugar and cotton plantations, which were huge fields full of crops that had to be picked every day. A few days before he was due to sail, John was sent by his father to Maidstone, in Kent, on some business, and was given permission to call at Chatham afterwards to visit the Catlett family, who had nursed his mother during her final illness.

The Catlett family made John very welcome and introduced him to their three oldest children: Jack, who was eleven, Elizabeth, who was thirteen, and Mary, or Polly as she was known, who was nearly fourteen. John fell in love with Mary immediately. He had no way of knowing that years earlier his mother and Mary's had hoped that their children might one day marry.

John had only meant to spend three days with the Catletts but could not bear to be parted from Mary and his stay increased to three weeks. He deliberately missed the ship to Jamaica, preferring to face his father's anger than not see Mary for years. John felt unable to explain to his father, when he finally did return to London, about his love for Mary.

Eventually his father calmed down and John was sent on a ship to Venice, in Italy. Unfortunately he fell again under the bad influence of the crew he was sailing with and began to forget about his efforts to live a better life. He began to slowly slide away from God once more.

At the same time worry was plaguing the British king, George II. The French navy, which was very powerful, was threatening British control of the English Channel and the king desperately needed more sailors in the Royal Navy to help protect it. Unfortunately no one wanted to join the navy because the pay was so poor and the sailors were treated very badly. As a result the law allowed naval captains to send out 'press-gangs' to get hold of men and bring them on board to join the crew. At the age of eighteen John found himself 'impressed' in this way and was taken on board H.M.S. *Harwich*.

Life was very hard aboard the *Harwich*, and not just for John. There was very little room for the crew of three hundred and fifty men and their living conditions were very cramped. Despite the fact that these men needed to be strong and fit to fight, the food was awful. The sea-cakes were full of maggots and the meat was so tough that the sailors were actually able to carve it into models and polish it. The cheese could be made into buttons and insects called weevils would crawl out of the biscuits. Drinking water was green and full of all kinds of creatures. Many of the sailors unsurprisingly died of disease. John was spared but received comfort only from the thought of Mary.

The captain of the *Harwich* knew John's father, and John was promoted to a better job and he began to bully and command the sailors he had once eaten his meals with. He made friends with a young man named Job Lewis and together they laughed at the Bible and mocked God. John was now separated from the Lord his mother had loved.

Early in the following year John learned that his ship was to be sent on special duties and would be away from home for five years.

John found the thought of being away from Mary for that long unbearable, and was desperate to avoid it. As the ship set sail from England a fierce storm forced it to shelter at Plymouth. John was sent ashore to guard a group of sailors and decided to run away. He was determined to go to his father and see if he would get him a better job somewhere else. However, deserting a ship is a very serious offence, and when John was just two hours away from his father, after walking for absolutely miles, he was captured by a group of soldiers and marched back to Plymouth. He was kept in the guardhouse for two days and then taken back on board H.M.S. *Harwich* to await his punishment.

By now John was in despair. His father was tired of his antics, and he could not believe that Mary would ever want him, and he had angered the captain so often on the voyage that he knew he could not expect mercy. Therefore it was no surprise when all the crew was ordered on deck to witness his humiliation. John was stripped to the waist and stood, legs apart, over a grating. His arms were spread out above his head, fixed at the wrists, and the ship's doctor stood ready. The captain read out John's crime and his punishment and, when the order was given to start, he was whipped mercilessly, until the captain gave the command to stop. John was carried below deck where the doctor, with hot tar or salt water, cleansed his wounds to stop the spread of infection. The doctor's care afterwards was almost as bad as the punishment itself.

For days John lay in his hammock, in agony. The other sailors were not allowed to speak to him and he had a long time to think. Alone and friendless, ill with fever, thoughts of his mother and Mary drifted through his mind as he sorrowed over his wasted life. He was tempted to throw himself into the sea and spent a long time planning how to kill the captain and then himself. Only the thought of Mary stopped him from any such wicked behaviour for sadly he no longer had any fear of God, nor did he love him.

The captain was as eager to be rid of John as John was to kill the captain and when a merchant ship met the *Harwich* and wanted to exchange two of its crew the captain immediately handed over John to be another captain's problem. Once on board the *Pegasus* John discovered that the captain and his crew were involved in the slave trade. They were heading out to the west coast of Africa to capture natives to sell to traders in the West Indies in return for ginger, sugar, rum, pearls and cotton to take back to Britain. The captain of the *Pegasus* also knew John's father and was kind to him for his sake. John had every opportunity for starting afresh but instead was worse than ever.

John's bad language and poor behaviour soon earned the captain's disgust, but John thrived on the attention the other sailors gave him. They made him a hero among them, especially after he made up a song about the captain and encouraged the crew to sing it as rudely and as often as possible. Soon the captain of the *Pegasus* hated John as much as the captain of the *Harwich* had. Years later John would remember his life with shame and wish earnestly that it could be "buried in eternal silence."

For six months John worked on the *Pegasus* in the slave trade, along the coast of Africa. Men, women and children were rounded up like cattle and crammed into tiny and filthy living quarters, chained so they could hardly move. Many died in the ship's hot and stinking hold and every morning more dead bodies were found among the few living, all chained together.

As the crowded ship was preparing to leave Africa the captain suddenly died. The first mate took charge of the ship, but John knew how much that man hated him too. It was very likely that he would be exchanged onto the first warship they passed so he decided to stay in Africa. The *Pegasus* sailed for the West Indies and John began to work for a slave trader called Clow, on the island of Benaroes.

Clow's wife, known by John as P.I., hated John and quickly turned Clow against him. A sudden and violent fever prevented

John from going on a trading trip with Clow and he was left with P.I. When he did not get better quickly she stopped looking after him and treated him badly. Frantic for food and drink, he was glad to receive scraps from P.I.'s plate, but one day he was so weak that he dropped the plate and lost the few scraps that he so desperately needed. P.I. simply laughed at him. Even the slaves, who were abused and mistreated, felt sorry for him. Sometimes, when John had the strength, he would crawl out at night and pull up roots from the plantation, eating them raw. He despaired to think what Mary would think of him.

Clow took John with him on his next voyage up river but wrongly accused him of stealing and treated him terribly. Whenever Clow left the ship John was locked on board with only a pint of rice to feed him through the day. The starving man was allowed to fish with Clow's leftovers for bait, and anything caught was eaten hungrily, whether it was burnt or raw. John now owned nothing but the clothes he was wearing, and he was kept on deck during heavy rain and blistering heat. He knew hunger, pain, cold and exhaustion. He had been completely broken but still did not think to turn to God. He wrote to his father in the hope that he would be able to help him, and also wrote to Mary, but with little hope of any of his letters reaching her.

After a year John found a job with another trader, who treated him better, and put him in charge of a factory with another white man. The two men were preparing to make a journey inland one day, when they were delayed. While they were waiting, John's work mate spotted a ship passing and sent up a smoke signal, asking for trade. Although not a usual trading place the captain decided to stop. The ship belonged to Joseph Manesty, the friend of John's father, who had asked Joseph to help find John, so the captains of all his ships had been ordered to look out for him. The captain of this ship, the *Greyhound*, was delighted to have found John, but he no longer wanted to leave Africa. In order to persuade him the

John worked at the pump tirelessly from three in the morning until midday and as he pumped he found himself thinking of God, and asking for His mercy

captain lied and told him that some money had been left to him. John was unsure for a while until he remembered Mary, in England, and his hope of marrying her. That settled it and he set sail on the *Greyhound*.

The *Greyhound* was trading for gold, ivory, wood and beeswax. These took a long time to collect and it was a year later and a thousand miles further up the coast before the ship stopped trading. Despite his escape from slavery, the captain's kindness and the thought of seeing Mary again, John still did not change his ways, and was further from God than ever.

John was soon to turn twenty-four and the *Greyhound* began to sail towards Brazil and from there to the banks of Newfoundland where she fished for cod. As March began the *Greyhound* picked up the strong westerly winds that would push her back to England. By now the ship was in a poor state of repair.

As John waited for England to come into sight he saw a book called *The Imitation of Christ* in the captain's cabin and began to read it. As he read about the glories of Christ he began to feel troubled that maybe everything he knew about God really was true. He knew he was a sinner but felt he was alone to suffer under the weight of his sin. That same day came the storm that convinced John Newton that God not only really existed, but truly cared for him, despite his sinful state.

Once free of the storm the crew faced starvation for there was very little food to eat. An error of judgement meant that a cloud mass was declared to be land and the crew ate all the remaining food in the expectation of being on land very soon. The wind became stronger and blew the ship away from Ireland and towards the islands of Western Scotland. The travelling was so hard that one of the crew members died. For some reason the captain blamed John for all these troubles and wanted to throw him overboard, as if he were Jonah, and hopefully save the ship. John felt awful because he thought maybe it was true and the ship's problems really were entirely his fault. Just in time, though, there was a change in the wind and the ship began to move in the right direction. The next morning, as the last food on board was being cooked the *Greyhound* anchored in Ireland.

John by now knew the gospel to be true and said that he "began to know there is a God, who hears and answers prayer." He was terribly sorry for his past life and very thankful for God's mercy upon him. He went to a church in Ireland and promised God that he would serve him all his life.

When the *Greyhound* was fit to sail the crew set off for Liverpool. Although John did not know it at the time, his father was also setting off from there to take up the job of Governor of York Fort, in Hudson Bay, Canada. Before he left, John's father visited Mary's family and gave his permission for John and Mary to marry if they wanted to. John never saw his father again and so was never able to tell him how sorry he was for all the trouble he had caused him because Mr Newton died in Canada two years later.

Joseph Manesty, in Liverpool, was very glad to see John again and was kind enough to offer John the command of one of his ships. However, John knew that he was not fit enough to be in charge of another voyage and instead agreed to go on the *Brownlow* as first mate, serving under another captain.

Before he sailed he went to Chatham to visit Mary although this first meeting made him feel very shy and awkward around her. He longed to tell her that he loved her but could only manage to ask if he could write to her while he was at sea. He felt that he would be able to be honest with her in writing. She assured him that she was not engaged to anybody else and would happily wait for him to return to her from his voyage on the *Brownlow*.

John set off again for the African coast but this time with a much happier heart. Unfortunately, away from other Christians and Bible teaching he found himself slipping into his old and bad ways again.

He struggled with his difficulties for many months and always failed to behave how he knew God wanted him to. He crept away to a quiet part of the island and prayed earnestly, telling God that he thought he could be a Christian. However, he was afraid that he would keep failing and let the Lord down. During these quiet moments when it was just him and God, John knew that he was only strong when he realised and admitted to being weak, and trusted in Christ to help him instead of relying on his own strength. John soon realised how unhelpful it was for him to be in such bad company as the other sailors every day and tried daily to go for a walk to be alone with God, talking and praying and praising him. These were probably his happiest times while in Africa.

The ship returned to Liverpool some months later and John immediately set off for Chatham. He had now known and loved Mary for seven years and upon this meeting she agreed to marry him. The wedding took place on February 1st, 1750 and although they were poor they were very much in love and very happy.

Six months later John was asked to be the captain of another ship, the *Duke of Argyle,* and although he did not want to leave Mary he agreed to go. It was obviously part of God's plan for him because he grew as a Christian and he was always able to say that he was pleased he had gone. He was a good captain, and treated his crew well, and kept a diary of his travels. He found it far more helpful to read Christian books than any others and so read nothing else. As he came to know and love God's word he understood more about how God wanted him to live. As captain he started services on Sundays aboard his ship and he brought about an order to his life, allowing eight hours a day for sleep, eight hours for exercise and devotion, and eight hours for his books. Many times he was aware of God's hand upon him, bringing him through many dangers, plots against him and illnesses, and he was very grateful that God could still look with favour and love upon him after all the trouble he had once caused.

He was fortunate enough to meet another Christian captain, called Alexander Clunie, who was a great help to John. They both had a month on the island of St. Christopher and spent each evening talking about following Jesus. Alex helped John to pray aloud and encouraged him to be bolder in speaking up about Jesus. He also gave helpful advice about churches in England. John was to think often of Alexander's help and advice as he sailed home, and thanked God for bringing him such a good friend.

He was delighted to be back with Mary but after only four months together he was to set sail on another slave-trading voyage. He was not happy about this, feeling that selling people as slaves did not agree with what he was learning from the Bible. He prayed, trusting that God would show him the right thing to do. God ended John's career in the slave trade by causing him to have a fit and fall unconscious for an hour just two days before the ship was due to sail. When John came round he was dizzy and in pain and the doctor decided it would be unsafe for him to sail and someone else took his job. The voyage was actually a disaster and many people on board died, so God had been very gracious to John.

As John recovered Mary became ill and they went to Kent to help her recover. John visited London and heard some wonderful preaching, but unfortunately they knew that they could not stay there forever.

Joseph Manesty was still a good friend and put John forward for a job as tide-surveyor in Liverpool, believing the post to be free. It turned out that somebody else already had the job and had no intention of giving it up but the very next day was found dead in his bed, and the job was John's. John returned to Liverpool and Mary joined him a while later, when she was better.

The more preaching John heard the more he and Mary grew as Christians and he began to wonder what God wanted him to do with the remainder of his life. He knew that his mother had always prayed that he would become a minister and he wondered if this was God's plan for him.

He applied to the Archbishop of York, who turned him down, so John knew he must trust God to work in his own time. He slowly began to preach in chapels, and although his first few times were awful he learnt from his mistakes. People were helped by his ministry and he started to be asked to preach in other places. A while later he was ordained a minister in the Church of England and was asked to go to the town of Olney, near Northampton, in 1764.

It was quite a contrast to his past life to be sent to one of the poorest towns in the country, many miles inland. The people there were hardworking with the men spending their days farming the land and the women and young girls making lace for up to ten hours a day. These people knew what it was to be hungry and there was often illness in the village, and they were so poor that often a group of lace-makers would gather in one room so that they could share the light from one candle. John and Mary ministered to these people and soon loved them. All were welcome at their home and John could often be found praying, reading, writing in his study or giving helpful advice to his parishioners. The people loved Mary and when she had to leave the village for a while to tend her sick father they prayed for her quick return to them.

John often felt uncomfortable in the pulpit but his love for God shone through his preaching. He told a student that God had sent him to Olney not to become a "ready speaker, but to win souls for Christ." He prepared his sermons by writing notes but never took them into the pulpit with him. His sermons were not long for he believed it better for the villagers to hear the word of God little and often rather than for ages, when they were likely to lose interest. This way it was a joy for them to hear the Bible read and explained, and to be able to understand the gospel clearly. John preached from the heart and so many people came to hear him that it was necessary to extend the church by building a gallery. The congregation grew in number but the people also had a serious desire to learn from the word of God. As well as morning and afternoon services on a Sunday a small group of people started coming to John's house after tea to pray. This group increased in number to about seventy and eventually their prayer meeting became an evening service where John also preached. Meetings for children and young people were also started, and the church people were divided into groups of about ten so that John could meet with each group for prayer and fellowship once every six weeks. Some members started another prayer meeting at six on a Sunday morning. Forty to fifty villagers would walk for many miles, through all weather, to meet with other Christians and seek God's face as early as they could on the Lord's Day. John was wonderfully used by God to reach many people in his time at Olney.

Three years after first arriving at Olney the Newtons' home was enlarged to help them cope with all their visitors. On Sundays, all those who had walked six miles or more to church were invited to stay for lunch and although it was difficult for Mary to feed so many guests on the little money they had, a good friend, John Thornton, urged them to continue welcoming people into their home and sent money to them regularly to help with their expenses.

In 1772 God blessed the people of Olney with revival and many became concerned about the state of their souls. People asking questions often kept John busy after the services, and although he was exhausted he was thankful that they all wished to know God better. By now many people were also writing to him for advice and he was spending much time in his study replying to them all. In 1774 he published forty-one of his letters in a book called *Omicron*. He also began to write a book on church history and wrote many beautiful hymns. One of his closest friends in Olney was the poet, William Cowper, and together they produced a hymnbook called *The Olney Hymns* of which William wrote 68, and John 280. John's love of words and creativity, which had once been used to make up rude songs and unkind rhymes, were used by God to write many fine hymns. His best-known hymn begins:

Amazing grace! How sweet the sound!
That saved a wretch like me!
I once was lost, but now am found;
Was blind, but now I see!

John printed some of his sermons and also wrote his story, telling how God had saved him. Many people were helped and encouraged by his writings, realising that God would and could forgive anyone, no matter what they had done. Hundreds of people, inspired by his story, visited Olney to meet the sea captain that God had so wonderfully converted.

John also travelled to preach, and in the summertime he and Mary would set off, 'on tour', and visit different parts of the country, with John preaching where he could.

When John had been in Olney sixteen years he started to feel that he should move on. He was saddened that many people in Olney still did not believe, and as some of the older church members had died and the younger ones were not as taken with spiritual matters, John and Mary felt God was telling them that their time in Olney was coming to an end. They asked God for guidance and he opened the way for them to go to a church in London. In January 1780 John became the rector of St. Mary's Woolnoth and St. Mary's Woolchurch.

London was a dirty, noisy place then, with no organised police force to control the many fights that often broke out. John managed to find a suitable house in Charles Square, Hoxton, with trees in front and a field behind where cows grazed. Trouble was brewing as John settled into work and six months after he had

John preached from the heart and so many people came to hear him that it was necessary to extend the church by building a gallery

arrived in London, on Friday June 2, 1780, thousands of people marched into the city towards the Houses of Parliament headed by a Scottish Member of Parliament, Lord Gordon. He was a Protestant who had stirred up feeling against the Catholics because Parliament had been restoring privileges to them. The marchers surrounded the Houses of Parliament, threatening the Members inside and causing panic as swords were drawn and the mob spilled into the street to destroy Catholic properties. The next day the crowd reached Hoxton and burnt down a Catholic school. It was a sad fact that many of the protestors were not Protestants at all, but drunken idle people who had got caught up in the crowds and were now enjoying causing chaos. Soldiers were sent to various parts of the city but were ordered not to shoot, and realising this the mob soon took control. By the Tuesday evening Newgate and New Prison had been set on fire and all the prisoners released. The violence became worse as by the next day every prison in London, except one, was burnt and the prisoners freed. Many rioters were burnt to death in the fires they themselves had started but this did not stop the others. The king ordered out the guards and John could hear the guns firing all during the night. By the next morning the rioting had finally stopped and the fireman were attempting to put out the many fires. The streets were littered with broken bottles and casks, ruined buildings, and over two hundred dead bodies. John returned to his study and in a letter wrote simply, "we are well."

One of the most famous men to admire John Newton was William Wilberforce, the Member of Parliament for Hull. He had become a Christian and was increasingly concerned about the slave trade, even trying to get it stopped by getting the law changed. John was also concerned about the cruel way that slaves were treated, having witnessed it for himself, and he wrote a booklet called "Thoughts on the African Slave Trade" which Wilberforce had printed, sending thousands of copies across the country. The two men worked well together in their untiring efforts, and their attempts to stop such a shocking practice went on for many years. A law was finally passed in 1807 to stop slave trading but it was not until 1833 that all British-owned slaves were freed.

John and Mary never had any children of their own but two of their nieces lived with them at times, because their own parents had died. Eliza Cunningham died while living with them, which upset them terribly, but Elizabeth Catlett lived with them for many years and was able to support John when his beloved Mary died of cancer, ten years after they moved to London. She had struggled against it for two years but had been in much pain towards the end of her life and it was a blessed release for her to be with her Lord. She had been told by the doctor to live a quiet and peaceful life once she knew she had cancer but their home was always open to anyone who needed it and their wise and helpful conversation was always in demand. John was always grateful for Mary's love and support throughout his life. When she died, John said that it was as if "the world seemed to die with her." In his time of great sorrow John still knew God's strength and comfort. The following Sunday he preached on verses from Habakkuk, chapter 3, reminding himself and his listeners that whatever happens and whatever losses there may be in life, he was able to say, "yet I will rejoice in the Lord, I will joy in the God of my salvation."

As John grew older his strength began to fail him but he was still preaching when he was eighty years old, even though his friends told him to stop. John would reply, "What! Shall the old African blasphemer stop while he can speak?" At his great age he found it hard to hear clearly and his sight was failing him but Elizabeth and her husband were a great help to him. He died, aged eighty-two, seventeen years after Mary, knowing and proving the grace of God, and the power of God to save, even a wretch like him.

Salvation despite sickness

The courage of **David Brainerd**

In the eighteenth century Indians lived freely in the wastelands of North America and, sadly, they were a godless people, although many missionaries had tried to convert them. Many of them had their lives changed forever by a young, sick man who devoted his life to their salvation.

In 1718, Dorothy Brainerd gave birth to her third son, David, in Haddam, Connecticut, which is also in North America. David's parents were both from families of preachers and from the start of their lives David, his four brothers and his four sisters lived in a home where God was very much loved. The whole family went to church regularly and the children learnt to read the Bible and respect and love it as God's word.

God laid a burden on David's heart from a young age, and despite his happy childhood David was a serious boy, concerned about his soul and afraid of death. When he was eight his father, Hezekiah, died while away on business and when he was thirteen, David's mother died of an epidemic in Haddam. David lived with friends for four years after he became an orphan and then moved to his own farm on which he worked for another year. He was still worried about the state of his soul and longed to be a Christian, knowing that he was not pleasing to God. He would often read his Bible, and pray, and worship in church but he did not know the peace of true faith, unable to accept that he had to trust the Lord Jesus.

When he was twenty-one David went to live with an old family friend, Phineas Fiske, who was a pastor. David hoped that Phineas might be able to help him, and the older man advised that he stop meeting with younger people and mix instead with older, more

The whole family went to church regularly

serious and more godly people. David took his advice and all the people he met thought he was a good man but he still felt that he was far away from God and he was miserable.

It was a Sunday evening when David was blessed by God's presence. He was suddenly, finally, aware that none of his good deeds would ever be good enough for God, and that Jesus had done everything for him. Through Jesus' death David could know real life and at last he believed in Jesus Christ as the way to God. David gratefully accepted God's way of salvation and began his life anew as a Christian.

David continued to read and pray and worship but now it was done with greater joy because he knew he was saved. He had thought briefly about being a minister but now he started to consider it more seriously and later that year he started college at Yale. He was a shy young man and was fearful of letting God down while at college but he was sure of God's love for him and felt more confident. Once at college he found it hard to spend as much time in God's presence as he had before and he was saddened to see so many students living their lives for themselves and caring little for God. Most of the students were younger than David and not very serious about their studies. David worked hard and was one of the best students in the college.

While at college David caught measles and was so ill that he had to return to Haddam. In a way this was a blessing because he was able to spend more time with God. After three months he was able to return to Yale but he became ill again soon after. This time he had a disease in his chest, and he had to return home once more. Although he was allowed back to Yale after a few more months he never really recovered from his illness. David was glad of the time to be alone with God, praying and reading his Bible, although of course he disliked being so ill.

At the same time God was at work in America and many people were being converted. It was the time of the Great Awakening, and preaching was being blessed and Christianity was reviving. At Yale College regular prayer meetings were held and the lives of many students were changed. David was thrilled at the evidence of a real spiritual life among the students and he became a leader among those who supported the Revivalists.

Unfortunately, not everyone at Yale was pleased about what was happening. The college leaders were not happy with the new preaching and thought that there was too much excitement about the new movement. Because of this the students thought the leaders were unspiritual and this led to bad feeling between the two groups. To try and keep control the leaders imposed strict rules, and one of these stated that if anyone said anything against the spiritual state of a leader, they would have to make a confession before the whole college and if they did it again, they would be expelled.

David was by now top of his class and he continued to study hard despite his ill health. He was sorry that the leaders were not in favour of the new movement and unwisely said to a friend that one of the tutors 'had no more grace than a chair.' By saying this David had broken the most serious rule and he was overheard and reported to the Rector, Thomas Clap, who was Head of the college. Clap was very angry and told David that he would have to say sorry in front of the entire college. David apologised to the Head but felt that, as he had made the comment to a few friends, a public confession was unfair. As a result he was told he had to leave, and in the middle of his studies, David was expelled from college.

David was upset at this but came to realise that he had been wrong to speak of another person in such a way, for only God can judge a man's spiritual state. The preacher and writer, Jonathan Edwards, met David and was impressed by his calm and humble manner. The preacher did what he could to help David make amends with the college, but without success. God was precious to

David at this time and he longed to be even closer to him. David tried many times to make things right with the Head of Yale but when Clap finally decided that David could return and continue his studies it was too late for David was, by then, fully involved in the Lord's work.

After leaving college David met men who were concerned about reaching the Native Americans— or Red Indians as they were then called—with the wonderful news about Jesus as the saviour of a lost humanity. David began to pray for the Indians and ask for guidance if this was what God wanted him to do. He had been an encouragement to the students while at Yale, but now he was needed elsewhere, and David could see God working actively in his life.

In the autumn, when David was twenty-four, he received a letter asking him to go to New York to talk about the idea of working among the Indians. David knew then that this was what God wanted him to do. He sold his property and with the money from the sale he paid for another man to study at college and train for the ministry. He then left his family and friends, not knowing when he would see them again, if ever. He knew it would be hard, but God had called him and he had to follow.

David visited the Indians on Long Island and understood at once the difficulties he would face. White men had treated the Indians badly by stealing their land and selling them strong drink. The Indians now trusted no one but their own kind, and they all spoke different languages and worshipped many gods and spirits. David did not know how he could ever make them trust him or listen to the truth he brought.

In one year David travelled twelve hundred miles on horseback and preached sixty sermons in thirty-six towns. He learned more about himself and the needs of the Indians. He had been sad to witness division and difficulties among Christians but he knew God was preparing him for the way ahead.

David stopped at Stockbridge, where John Sergeant and his wife, Abigail, had lived among the Mohegan Indians for four years. Being able to pray and talk with them and listen to John's advice was refreshing and encouraging. He then rode twenty miles to Kaunameek and stayed with a Scotsman and his wife. His food was mainly oatmeal porridge, boiled corn and bread baked in the ashes, sometimes with a little meat and butter. He slept on a heap of straw and lodged in a little log room. His work was hard and he was lonely, but he took comfort in knowing he was where God wanted him. The Indians would listen politely as David preached but he felt discouraged that their lives were not changing.

David's twenty-fifth birthday, a few weeks later, was spent in prayer and fasting, and wandering in the woods, talking to God. He felt he was being tested and being made to live a hard life for the sake of the gospel. He found it hard to speak to the Indians because the language barrier was so wide but God led him to an Indian man, called John, who was fluent in English and Indian and became a great help to David. Deciding to set up a school in Kaunameek, David made John the schoolmaster. The Indian children who attended learned quickly and David was able to teach them some of the great Bible truths that were so important to him. He moved out of his log room and into a wigwam while he built a hut of his own, so that he could be alone with God whenever he wanted.

David often had to travel many miles, on horseback, to visit churches and the Mission leaders. Within a few days of each other two churches asked if he would be their pastor. He was tempted by the thought of living in a house, and it would certainly have been better for his health, for he was often ill, but he knew he had been placed among the Indians by God, and he chose to stay with them. He soon began to wonder if he should move on to another area, however, because many of the Indians had had to leave Kaunameek as white men were stealing their land and forcing them to move westwards. He persuaded the Indians still left in Kaunameek to move to Stockbridge where John Sergeant could help them. The Indians David had been working with were sorry to lose him but he reminded them that other Indians needed to hear the gospel too. David had believed that not much had been done for God in Kaunameek but the reluctance of the Indians to let him go made him realise that his time had not been wasted.

David was told by the Mission to go to the Forks of the Delaware, hundreds of miles further west. He was twenty-six years old and still very weak but he willingly set off on the difficult journey, first by horse, and then across the Hudson River, and then a further hundred miles west through dangerous country.

It was very difficult bringing God to the Indians at the Forks of the Delaware. They were scattered throughout the region and had their own religious leaders who threatened to poison anyone who accepted Christ. They, too, were suspicious of white people because of the way they had been treated, but David kept praying for them. He then heard of Indians in the Susquehanna region, and felt he had to tell them about Jesus too. He made another dangerous journey on horseback through wild lands, until his horse broke its leg and had to be killed; and he then continued on foot for days. He was able to preach to the Indians but they were not interested in what he had to say. He returned to the Forks of Delaware but after a year there he felt he had done little more good than he had achieved at Kaunameek. He had not seen one Indian turn to Christ after two years of living among them, and he began to believe that he was a burden to the Missionary Society. He decided he would try for one more year and if he still had no success he would give up his position.

Although David was disappointed that he had not helped any Indians to salvation, his faith remained strong and he was rewarded for this when he travelled to Crossweeksung, eighty-five miles south. The Indians here were scattered too but he preached

The Indians would listen politely as David preached, but he felt discouraged that their lives were not changing

to a few women and children who then travelled themselves for fifteen miles to tell others of the white man who spoke of Jesus the Saviour. Every day more people came to hear him preach and listened to what he said with great interest. He was asked to preach twice a day and happily accepted, knowing that God was at work in the people's lives.

After two weeks he felt he ought to go back to the Forks at Delaware. The Indians at Crossweeksung begged him to return soon and promised to live together so that he could preach to them all. He promised he would return as soon as he could, and left, hoping they would not forget what he had told them. Upon his arrival at the Forks of Delaware he was delighted to learn that his interpreter there, a man called Moses, had trusted Christ. David had the joy of baptising him and was thrilled in having a Christian interpreter.

David returned to Crossweeksung as he had promised and saw that God really was at work there. As he preached the love of Christ his listeners cried as they realised that they did not know this love and were far away from God. People of all ages wept as they saw themselves as God saw them, and they fell to the ground, crying and praying that God would forgive them and change their hearts. As the summer passed, more and more Indians were affected by David's preaching and many trusted Jesus for their salvation. A young woman came to listen, planning only to mock David, but instead the Holy Spirit moved within her and she lay on the ground for hours, praying.

Within a month, there were ninety-five people regularly listening to David's preaching. Twenty-five people said that they were Christians and their lives showed a real difference. David baptised them, reminding them that they were to live for God. As the months passed the number of believers grew, and they were known for their love of God and each other.

David, encouraged by this success, began to think again of the

Indians of the Susquehanna and wondered if they would listen to him this time. He still had a weak chest and was not a strong man at all, but he prepared to make the long journey westwards again. He rode through terrible storms, and could hear wolves howling nearby at night, but God kept him safe. David met the Nantichokes, a tribe of Indians who were feared by the other tribes. David watched as they performed a special sacrifice and was troubled by how godless they were. The Nantichokes sacrificed deer and threw deer fat into the fire, making the flames leap, dancing and screaming wildly all the while. David gave thanks that he had been saved from a life without Jesus and prayed that God would do something for the lost Indians.

Back at Crossweeksung, David was a spiritual father to the new believers and he taught them from the Bible how God wanted them to live. He told them about the Lord's Supper, a special service where Christians look at their lives and at what God has done for them and take bread and wine as symbols of Jesus' body and blood being given for his people. The Indians were eager to learn all about Jesus and were pleased to take part in such an important service. David was thrilled to see how many of the Indians were growing as Christians and he was able to baptise more that had been converted, and enjoy the love they had for one another, as children of God.

Unfortunately the Indians at Crossweeksung were forced to move around because the ground was not good for growing crops. David felt that if they could settle in one place it would be easier for them to attend services. A good piece of land was chosen fifteen miles away, at a place called Cranberry. The Indians began clearing the land and two months later, after they had moved there, a school was opened and a teacher found. A small house was also built for David to live in while he worked among them.

When he was twenty-eight David had to decide about his immediate future. He was pale, thin and weak and needed to rest if he hoped to live for very much longer. He did not know if his increasingly poor health was God's way of encouraging him to stay at Cranberry and serve the Indians there as their pastor, or if he should continue to make difficult journeys to reach other Indians to tell them of Christ. David prayed, as he always did during times of indecision. He realised that God had used his whole life to prepare him for a hard and lonely time on earth, and nothing could compare with the delight of following God and obeying his will. He felt that God was calling him to take the message of the gospel to faraway Indian tribes and he soon set off again, this time with six Indians.

He was very ill on the journey, and often in great pain, but he rode on, determined to be obedient to his Lord. God gave him strength and he preached with power. The Indians seemed to think carefully about what he said, and were impressed by his devotion, and David believed that the journey was not wasted and that God would use it for good. He then returned to Cranberry and continued to preach, even though he was so weak he could hardly stand. After some months he journeyed to New Jersey and preached when he was strong enough. He saw his brother John, who was also a Christian, and was pleased when John left for Cranberry to work among the Indians in David's place.

David travelled on to the home of his friend, Jonathan Edwards. He was now very ill and he stayed with his friends, and was looked after by Jerusha, Jonathan's daughter. He was so weak he had to stay in bed. He was not afraid of death, and looked forward to being in heaven with Jesus, where there would be no pain and where he could leave his sinful state behind. He died in Jonathan's home, aged only twenty-nine. Many people were thankful for his short life, particularly the Indians, 'his people', whom he had loved so much and for whom he was willing to live such a hard life that they might learn about Christ.

David had kept a diary and Jonathan Edwards had it printed. It

He prepared to make the long journey westwards again

spoke of David's walk with God and it was clear to see how God had worked within him. David Brainerd was a man who wanted to give everything to God. He knew that nothing was more important than following the Lord Jesus, and devoted his life to helping other people—who might have died in ignorance—learn that glorious truth too.

Running with God

The story of Olympic athlete **Eric Liddell**

"I'm not running."

It was a simple statement but it shocked and amazed the world. Eric Liddell, Scotland's best athlete, had been chosen to run for Britain in the 1924 Olympic Games, and had a very good chance of winning. The only problem was that the heats were on a Sunday and Eric—as a Christian—always kept Sundays special, worshipping in church, listening to preaching and meeting other Christians. Sunday was the Lord's day and Eric was not prepared to waste a moment of it. His devotion to God led to many people feeling betrayed by him. They thought Olympic glory should come before anything—even before God. Newspapers wrote cruel things about Eric, and he was accused of being mean and selfish, and letting his country down. Even his teammates tried to change his mind but Eric was unmoved. He did receive support from many athletes who admired his loyalty to God. Eric's decision meant that there were a number of races he could not run in but he did not waver. This incident, and indeed his whole life, revealed a man with an unswerving devotion to the Lord.

Eric was born in 1902, in China, to Mary and James Liddell, missionaries from Scotland. China at that time was a dangerous country, counting all foreigners as enemies. Eric's parents were concerned for the safety of him and his older brother, Robert. When Eric was born, his parents were living in the port of Tientsin, but his father was sent to the village of Siaochang, in the Great Plain of northern China. Once Eric was old enough to endure the difficult two-day journey his mother took him and his brother to join their father.

The mission station in Siaochang was enclosed within a high

wall, keeping the houses, schools and church safe. Eric's sister, Jenny, was born there and they all played with the Chinese children. As a child, Eric suffered an illness that left his legs very weak, and there were fears that he would never be strong enough to run like a normal little boy.

When he was five the family returned to Scotland for a year. It was strange for the children to see the lochs and mountains of Drymen after being so used to the dry yellow plains in China. Eric's grandfather was the village grocer and the villagers made his son and family feel very welcome. Robert and Eric started at the village school, fascinating the other children who thought at first that they were Chinese. Soon they were all friends, with the Liddell boys teaching the other children Chinese games and learning Scottish ones themselves.

The year was soon over but it was decided that Robert and Eric should remain in Britain to continue their schooling. James returned to China, and Jenny and her mother went with the boys to London, staying in a small house next to the School for the Sons of Missionaries for a few months, until Eric and Robert had settled in. They said goodbye to their mother in the office of the head-master, and she returned to her husband in China, not knowing when she would see her sons again.

At age six Eric was pale and small but his headmaster was keen on fresh air and sport and Eric began to grow into a healthy, strong boy. He loved rugby and cricket, and captained both teams when older. He became very good at athletics and spent more time on the sports field than in lessons. Robert was also a keen sportsman and the brothers were often rivals. Their sporting prowess can be seen in the Sports Day results when Eric was sixteen and Robert was eighteen (See top of page 58).

Eventually Eric had to leave the school and he returned to Scotland where his mother, Jenny, and younger brother Ernest had rented a house ready for James Liddell's return from China.

It was strange for the children to see the lochs and mountains of Drymen

Cross Country Run	1 R.V. Liddell	2 E.H. Liddell
Long Jump	1 E.H. Liddell	2 R.V. Liddell
High Jump	1 R.V. Liddell	2 E.H. Liddell
100 Yards*	1. E.H. Liddell	2 R.V. Liddell
(EQUALLED SCHOOL RECORD OF 10.8 SECONDS)		
Hurdle Race	1 R.V. Liddell	2 E.H. Liddell
Quarter Mile	1 E.H. Liddell	2 R.V. Liddell

* 100 YARDS = 91.7 METRES

Robert was already at Edinburgh University, studying to be a doctor, and Eric was soon able to join him there to study science.

At university Eric's friends soon noticed his capabilities on the sports field and urged him to enter for the Athletic Sports. At first Eric insisted he was too busy but gradually his love of running meant that he began training for the 100 and 220-yard races. When the University Sports were held Eric won the 100 yard final, beating G. Innes Stewart, who was hoping to become a Scottish champion. Soon after this Innes only just beat Eric in the 220-yard race—the only race Eric ran in Scotland that he did not win.

Eric was given a place on the Edinburgh University team for the Scottish Inter-University Sports and he was obliged to do some serious training. He quickly learnt the importance of warming up properly and his performance improved. He was soon winning every race he entered. When he was twenty-one he broke the Inter-Universities record for the 440-yard race, and it was not broken again for another thirty-four years. He won so many trophies and prizes that he had difficulty finding space for them all.

During his second winter at the university Eric was asked to play rugby and had soon gained a place in the first team. He went on tour with his team to the south of England, and his skill and speed were so impressive that he was chosen to play for Scotland in international matches. He played against France, Wales and Ireland in his first season. After his second season he decided to leave the game so that he could devote more time to practising his running.

Eric was popular among the other athletes. He would always shake hands with his rivals and wish them the best, and although he enjoyed winning it did not make him so driven as to be unpleasant. In the time that he was running there were no starting blocks and the runners had to dig holes to place their feet in. Eric would lend his trowel to any runner without one, and would always speak to anyone who looked lonely. He once offered to change places with a less experienced runner who had been given the outside lane; there were no staggered starts so the odds were against the runner on the outside, but Eric offered to change despite this. It was easy to see why he was so well liked. Even those who lost to him could not grudge him his success.

Soon after this Eric's parents and two younger siblings returned to China, and the older boys moved into the Edinburgh Medical Mission Hostel. Robert was helping out with meetings in central Scotland, which were run by Christian students who were eager to tell others about Jesus. Eric was by now the best-known athlete in Scotland and the students thought it would be a good idea if Eric could speak at one of the meetings for men. A friend actually hitchhiked to Edinburgh to ask him and Eric immediately agreed.

God used this opportunity as an important point in Eric's life. Although a Christian, Eric had always been very quiet about his faith. At school he had gone to the weekly Bible classes but contributed little to the discussions. He had become a church member at fifteen but was still shy about speaking. He agreed to speak at the meeting because he knew that his faith was real and that God would give him strength when he needed it.

There were about eighty men at that meeting in Armadale in central Scotland. Eric, admittedly, was not a good speaker, but he spoke simply and lovingly about the God who meant so much to him; the God who could change lives, give faith to live and the power to run. The men listened carefully to his words, and many were touched by his faith that night.

Eric was asked to speak at more meetings after that and many people went along to hear him. They responded to his honesty, his friendliness and his evident love for God. Everyone who met him spoke highly of him. Eric was kept busy between his speaking engagements and athletic training but he made sure he studied hard too.

Selectors were beginning to watch athletes, ready to choose those who seemed promising for the 1924 Olympic Games. In July 1923, Eric ran in London for the first time. He won the 100 and 220-yard races in excellent times. The following week he ran for Scotland against England and Ireland at Stoke-on-Trent and won all three of his races. The last and longest—the 440-yard race—cemented his reputation as an athlete of incredible speed. As the race began another runner knocked him off the track. He stopped, thinking he would not be allowed to continue, but saw the officials waving him on. He began running again, although already twenty yards behind the others, and unlikely to catch up. Amazingly, he began to run harder and faster, and caught up with the leaders. With only forty yards to go he was third, but with a tremendous effort he burst into the lead and won the race. He collapsed in exhaustion but could hear the ecstatic cheers of the crowd as he was carried from the field.

Technically, Eric's style of running should have prevented him from ever winning a race, for he ran with his head thrown back, his knees up and his arms waving all over the place. Undeniably, though, he gave his all when he ran, and he invariably won.

After his spectacular show in London he was chosen to run for Britain in the Olympic Games, being held in Paris. He was to run in the 100 and 200 metre races, being already the 100-yard British champion. It was then that he stated his refusal to run in the heats—his wish to keep Sunday holy was stronger than his desire to win gold in Paris.

British hopes now rested on Harold Abrahams, a Jewish student from Cambridge University. He was fast but there were some very good American runners participating too.

Eric was asked instead to train for the 400-metre race. He had already shown he could run it but had never thought of it as his race. Britain was relying on Guy Butler, who had won the silver medal in the Olympic Games four years earlier.

Forty-four nations took part in the Paris Games in July 1924. Even as the Games started, Eric was still being asked to reconsider running in the 100-metre race, but on the Sunday during the heats he was preaching at a Scottish church in Paris.

Harold Abrahams managed to take gold for Britain and Eric cheered him as hard as anyone else. The following Tuesday Eric ran in the 200 metre heat and won a place in the final the next day. The USA won gold and Eric took the bronze medal when he came in third.

The day after, he entered the heats for the 400-metre race. He ran in three races, running faster every time, and got a place in the final. The morning of the final he was handed a note, signed by the man who massaged the British athletes. It read: 'In the old book it says, "He that honours me I will honour." Wishing you the best of success always.' The message was from a verse in the book of 1 Samuel, chapter 2, verse 30. This was of great encouragement to Eric.

The evening of the race Eric shook hands with the other five runners, as was his custom, before taking his place in the outside lane. Unexpectedly, the Scottish pipe-band began playing the tune 'The Campbells are Coming'. Once the tune finished the race started and Eric set an unbelievable pace. It seemed impossible to all the people watching that he would be able to keep up such a speed. After sprinting 200 metres Eric was in the lead with the American Horatio Fitch just two metres behind him. As the runners entered the final stretch it was usual for them to all start slowing down but Eric actually began to run faster. With his head back and his arms flailing Eric increased his lead and won the race five metres ahead of the American. Eric not only won the gold medal; he set a world record time of 47.6 seconds.

The crowd was deafening in its delight when Eric took his place to receive his medal. When it was over Eric quietly slipped out of the stadium. He had a speaking engagement the following Sunday in a Parisian church and he needed to prepare. Even at a time of glory and praise Eric did not forget about spreading the word of God.

Years later, a journalist asked Eric how he kept up such a speed when he ran with such a strange style. Eric gave the now famous answer: "The secret of my success over the 400 metres is that I run the first 200 metres as hard as I can. Then, for the second 200 metres, with God's help, I run harder."

Soon after Eric's victory two of his professors in Edinburgh were discussing how to make his graduation—taking place the following Thursday—special for the Olympic hero. Although many other people graduated that Thursday they all knew that it was really Eric's day. As he stepped forward to receive his Bachelor of Science degree, the audience stood up as one and cheered him. When the applause finally stopped the principal told everyone that in the ancient Olympic tests the victor was always crowned with wild olives and given a poem written especially in his honour. An olive wreath was placed on Eric's head and he was given a poem, written in Greek, on a scroll. Outside the hall, after the ceremony, students carried Eric in a sedan chair to St Giles Cathedral for the graduation service. The consideration and generosity of his friends overwhelmed Eric.

At the cathedral more people had gathered and Eric was asked to make a speech. After the graduation lunch Eric was asked to speak yet again before being taken, with the principal, for a tour of the city, surrounded by hundreds of students, before returning to

Eric increased his lead and won the race

the principal's house for tea. It was unquestionably an unforgettable day for the people of Edinburgh.

The next day there was yet another dinner in Eric's honour. He became very embarrassed hearing so many people praising him. He was asked to make a speech but this time what he said stunned his listeners, for he told them he was going to be a missionary in China.

He realised that he needed to know more about the Bible before he could start and so enrolled at the Scottish Congregational College in Edinburgh. He was willing to do anything necessary to prepare himself for God's work. During his studies he already had a job waiting for him in Tientsin, where he was born, at the Anglo-Chinese College. He would teach science, be in charge of athletics and share in the Christian teaching.

In July 1925, a year after his 'crowning', crowds in Edinburgh again surrounded Eric, this time to see him to the train station. He was carried in a decorated carriage by students from the college to the station, stopping the traffic in the city centre. Everybody was emotional as Eric, a hero, left Scotland for the last time.

The Tientsin Eric arrived in was very different from the city he had left as a small boy. It really was two cities - the old Chinese city, teeming with sailors, factory workers and peasants, and full of mosques and temples where Muslims and Buddhists worshipped. The new city was full of Japanese and European people who had won the land from the Chinese in a series of wars. Unsurprisingly, the Chinese disliked the foreigners living in their city.

The London Missionary Society ran the Anglo-Chinese College. They had their base in the French part of the city. Eric moved into the house where his family lived and prepared to start work at the college. Things did not quite go according to plan, since when he arrived most of the students were out on strike. Fortunately, as the term started again they gradually returned. There were five hundred pupils, mainly from wealthy Chinese families. The Mission hoped to train future leaders, providing them with a fine education and a sound Christian teaching. The College was a leader in sports at that time in China and believed sport to be an important part of the students' training. Eric knew that God had sent him to the best place, where all his strengths and talents could be used to full advantage.

Every morning, the College had a service, and Eric soon became the favourite speaker. Each week he would bring his students home for a Bible class. Although he loved children, and enjoyed talking and laughing with them, telling them stories and helping them run, Eric was not particularly comfortable teaching in a classroom. He taught best by his example, but still worked hard at his job and slowly became a better teacher. He naturally took charge of the college athletics and soon had the students breaking records. He did some running himself, against foreign troops, and played rugby with them. He organised the building of a sports ground in Tientsin and was one of the first to compete there at the Annual International Athletic Games. Few people in Britain knew of his continuing sporting success in China.

Eric earned himself the nickname 'The Flying Scotsman' when he managed to catch a boat against all the odds. He was running in an athletics contest at Darien and had to catch the boat back to Manchuria at three in the afternoon. He was entered to run in the 200 metre race which was an early race, but was then asked to run in the 400 metre race which was just thirty minutes before the boat set out, the port being twenty minutes away from the track. Eric ordered a taxi to wait for him at the finishing line. He was first through the line and simply kept running to meet the taxi. Suddenly the band started playing the national anthem, in favour of him, the British winner. Eric stopped and stood still respectfully while the tune was played. As soon as it finished he dashed towards the taxi, only to stop again as the French national anthem—the 'Marseillaise'—was played in honour of the Frenchman who came second. He finally leapt into the taxi and they sped off for the boat. As they arrived Eric saw that the boat had already left. As he watched in disappointment a wave caught the boat and threw it a little way back towards him. Eric threw his bags onto the deck of the boat and then leapt after them. Witnesses to this spectacle claimed he leapt fifteen feet from shore to boat—nearly five metres. With his natural modesty Eric denied the distance had been that great.

After Eric's parents returned to Scotland many friends were willing to stay with him to keep him company. They all described that time as a very rich period in their lives, for Eric never spoke unkindly of anyone, had a wonderful sense of fun and never dodged his tasks when there was work to be done.

A short time later Eric met a young girl called Florence MacKenzie, known by everyone as Flo. Her parents were missionaries from Canada and they soon became engaged and she then returned to Canada to train as a nurse. She later explained that Eric was able to live such a gentle and loving life because he believed in the power of prayer. He started each day by talking to God and reading his Bible, and committing the day to him. This gave him the strength to live each day for God. Eric returned to Scotland for a brief time before his marriage where a huge 'welcome home' meeting was held in Edinburgh, showing that the people of Scotland had not forgotten their hero.

He was immediately asked to speak at meetings in England, Scotland and Northern Ireland. He still believed strongly in keeping Sunday special and at one meeting in Edinburgh, he called on all young people's groups to think carefully about the growing use of Sunday for sports and games and the harm it might cause as people slipped away from God to play sport.

Eric and Flo were married in Tientsin, four years after they were first engaged. They set up home in Eric's house. A while later their first daughter, Patricia, was born. Soon after Eric was asked to go

Eric threw his bags onto the deck of the boat and then leapt after them

to Siaochang, where he had grown up, because there were not enough missionaries based there. Eric and Flo prayed about it and at first thought Eric should remain at the college but he knew that it was right for him to go. This meant he had to leave his wife and daughter, and new baby, Heather, for some months, but Eric knew he was living for God and not for himself and after twelve years in Tientsin he prepared to leave.

Eric's brother Robert was already working as a doctor in the mission hospital in Siaochang, and Eric joined him there. Everyone was suffering because of war and drought and all the people were in need of aid. Japan had recently invaded China, there was continual fighting and the hospital was constantly over-crowded and short-staffed.

Eric was given a huge area to cover, with churches to be visited and preached in, people to be cared for and Chinese preachers to be encouraged. The people there immediately loved Eric and his concern for their needs was obvious. He saved the life of one man who had been left for dead by Japanese soldiers, who had been beheading people in a village. One man had a gash from the back of his neck to his mouth and was laid in an outbuilding by other villagers for several days with dirty rags around his throat. Eric took him on the dangerous, eighteen-mile long journey to the mission hospital where he was saved. The man later became a Christian, and because he was an artist he painted pictures to show his gratitude.

By now life in Tientsin was very dangerous and Eric took his family to Canada and then Scotland, glad to leave China for a while. With the Second World War now broken out the Western part of the world was not much safer. Britain was now at war with Germany, Italy and then Japan. Eric offered to be a pilot in the RAF but was turned down and instead offered a job behind a desk. He decided he had more important work to do in China, and that that was where God wanted him to be, so the following year the family returned to China. Other ships travelling with them were torpedoed and sunk and Eric's ship had to travel faster because of the danger, causing its passengers to be very sick, but by God's grace they arrived safely in Tientsin, and Eric was able to return to Siaochang.

Conditions in Siaochang were far worse than when he had left. A high wall had been built around the entire village and from his room Eric could see exhausted men being forced to make a road. There was fierce fighting between the Chinese and Japanese and the villagers lived in fear. The missionaries knew that they would not be able to stay in the village for much longer and indeed, at the beginning of the next year they were told they had two weeks to leave Siaochang. Eric returned to Tientsin and heard later that Siaochang had been destroyed.

Eric grew more concerned for the safety of his family, especially since Flo was expecting their third child. They decided that she should take the children and go to Canada while Eric stayed in China. It was a difficult decision for them to make, and they hoped they would only be separated for a year or two. They could not have known that they would never see each other again.

Four months later, in Canada, Flo had a baby girl, Maureen. Eric was delighted when he heard the news. He was still living in Tientsin and had to stay in the city with the other missionaries because the fighting made it difficult for anyone to travel. So that his time there would not be spent idly Eric wrote a book which he hoped would help the Chinese pastors. By the end of the year Japan had joined the Second World War and within weeks the members of the London Missionary Society had to leave their homes in the French part of the city and stay with members of the English Methodist Mission in the British part of Tientsin. They were not allowed to go outside the area, and were not allowed to meet in groups of more than ten people, meaning that they could not have church services. To combat this Eric asked a different minister to prepare a sermon each week and ministers' wives would invite people round to tea on Sundays—never more than ten at a time—and copies of the sermon would be passed around and a short service held. This gave the missionaries strength and the certainty that God was with them. By the end of that year, however, life in Tientsin was becoming even more difficult and little news from China was reaching the West. No one knew what the Japanese would do next.

The following spring Eric and hundreds of other foreigners were ordered to go to the Civil Assembly Centre at Weihsien, south of Peking. They were not officially prisoners of war, but were instead 'civil internees'. The camp they were sent to was a ruined American mission station, not big enough to house the one thousand and eight hundred people who arrived, exhausted and emotional after a long train journey. The buildings in the camp had been wrecked and the place stank. Misery was rife as the internees had to join a long queue for supper to be given just a bowl of thin soup and some bread.

The internees began to take a role in the running of the camp, cleaning it and trying to make the most of it. There was a twice-daily roll call to make sure no one had escaped and find out who had died. With food so poor the people became dangerously thin and were always hungry. There were many arguments, with so many different people living in such cramped conditions. The business people did not care for the missionaries, and the missionaries, unfortunately, did not always like the business people. Eric was one of the few people that everybody in the camp did like and he was often asked for his advice. He was always busy, helping the young people maintain their studies, running sports, collecting supplies, cleaning, mending sports equipment and running the Christian fellowship. He was the chief translator for the Japanese and was also made warden of Blocks 23 and 24, but he was never too busy to see or help anyone who needed him. He also taught the Bible class on Sundays and although he was not a brilliant preacher people listened because of his obvious love for God and the way that his whole life was a testimony to that love.

Unfortunately the lack of food, the poor conditions and the hard work began to affect Eric. His friends noticed that he was slowing down in his activities and he began to suffer from bad headaches. He went to the camp hospital but the right equipment was not available and he could not be examined properly. He did seem to get better and tried to help in the camp but his strength was completely gone. At the age of forty-three he died from a growth on his brain. He told a nurse, just before he died, that it was "complete surrender". He did not give in; he just let God's will take first place over his own, as he had always done. His whole life was an example of a man who wanted to let God have his way unchallenged. He was willing to submit to that will in any way, even if it meant not running on a Sunday. With his death, by God's will, Eric's final race was over.